Pre-K 5

W0099589

Feelings

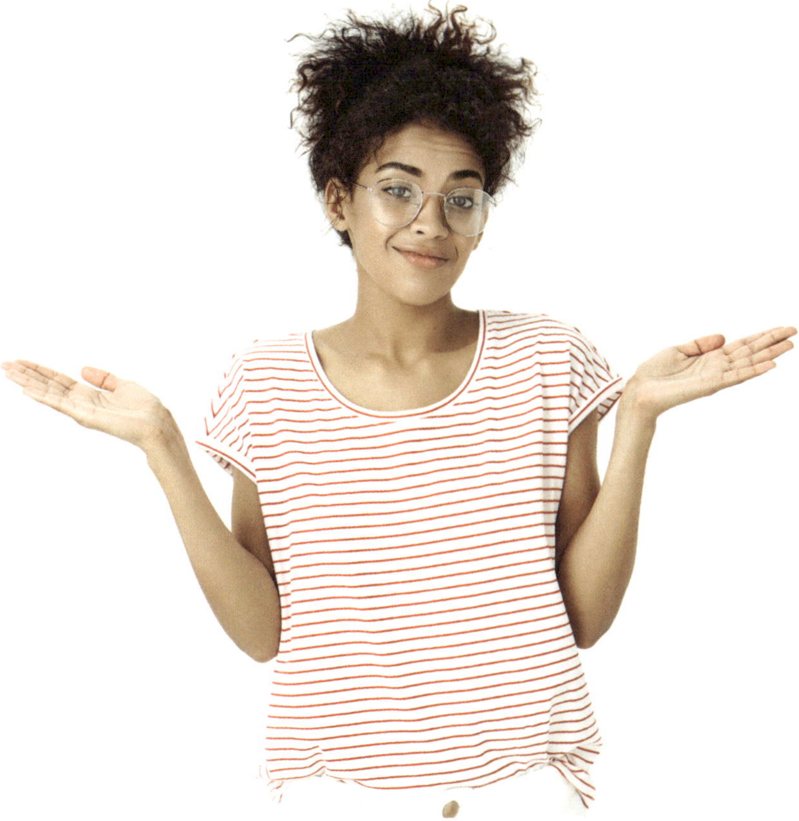

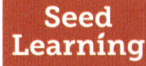

Seed Learning

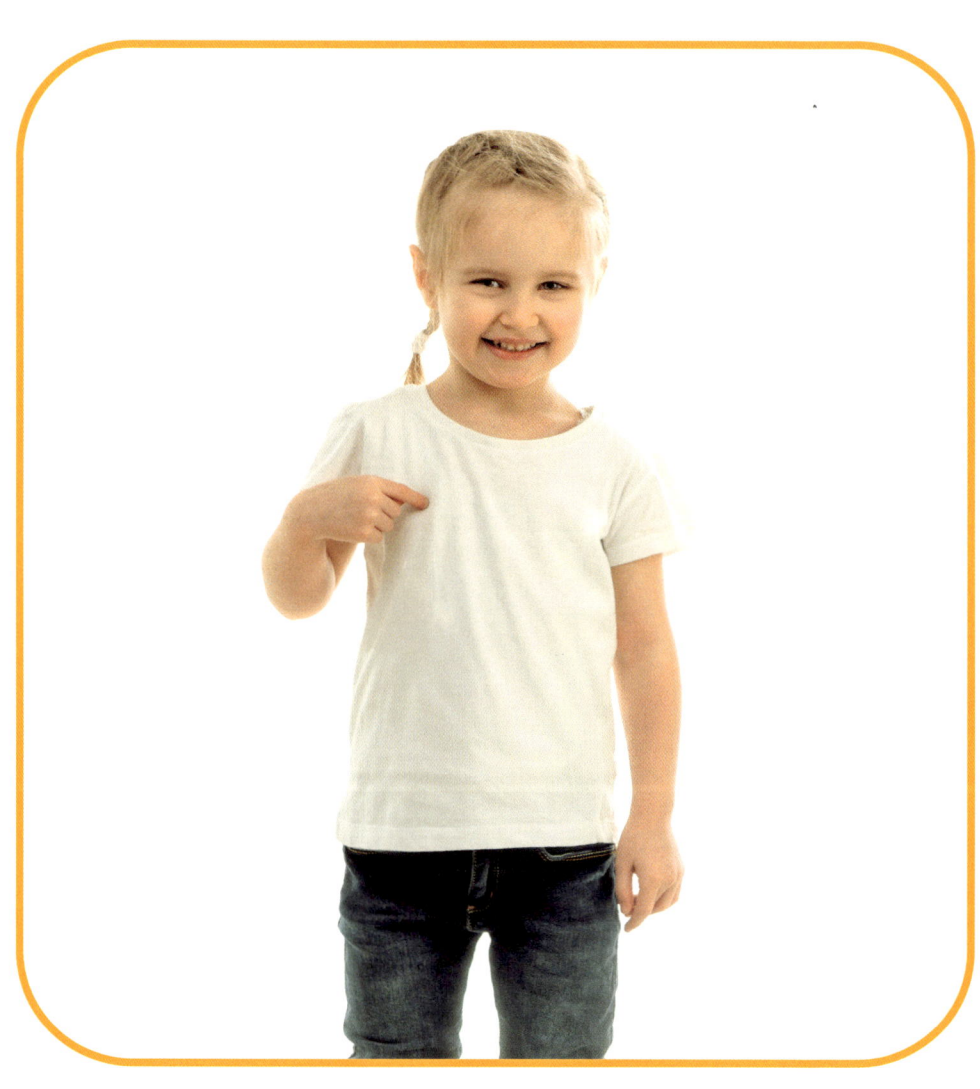

I

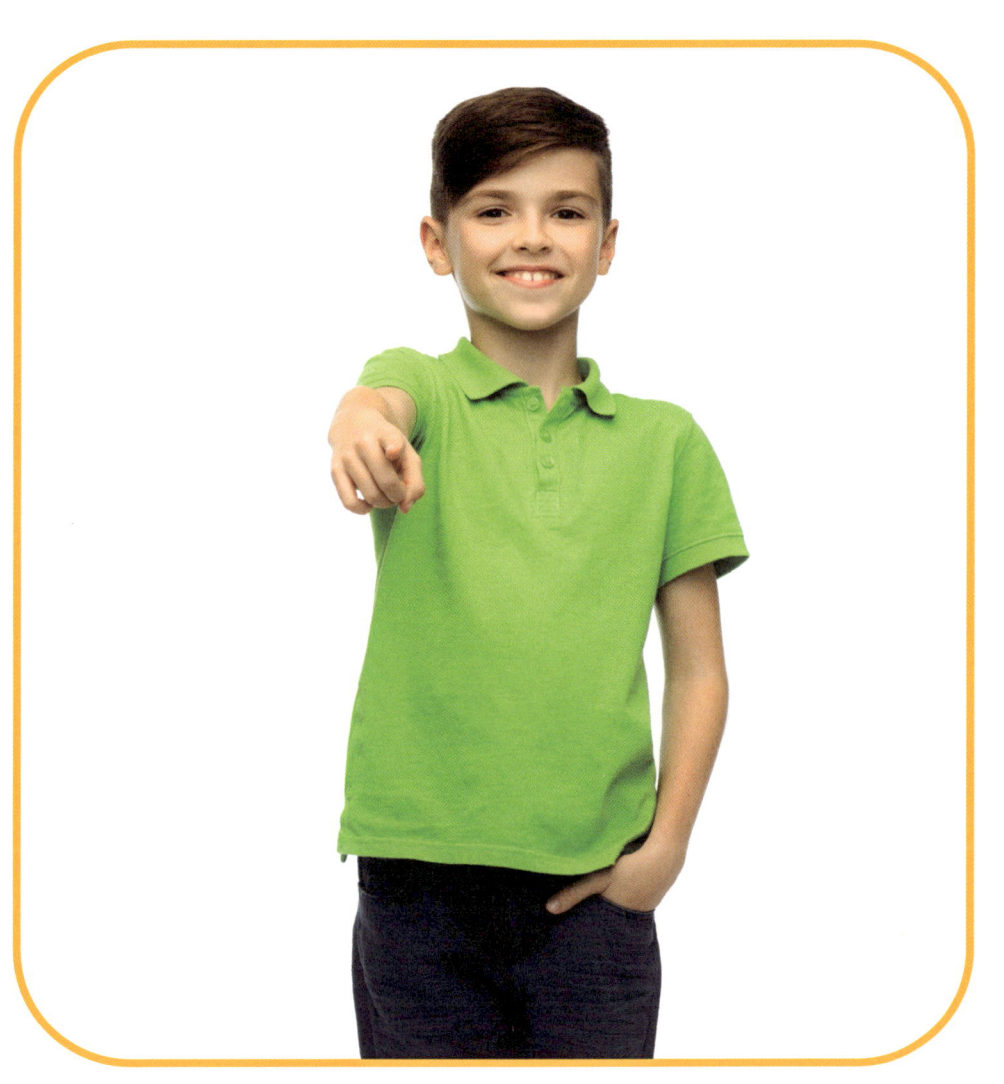

you

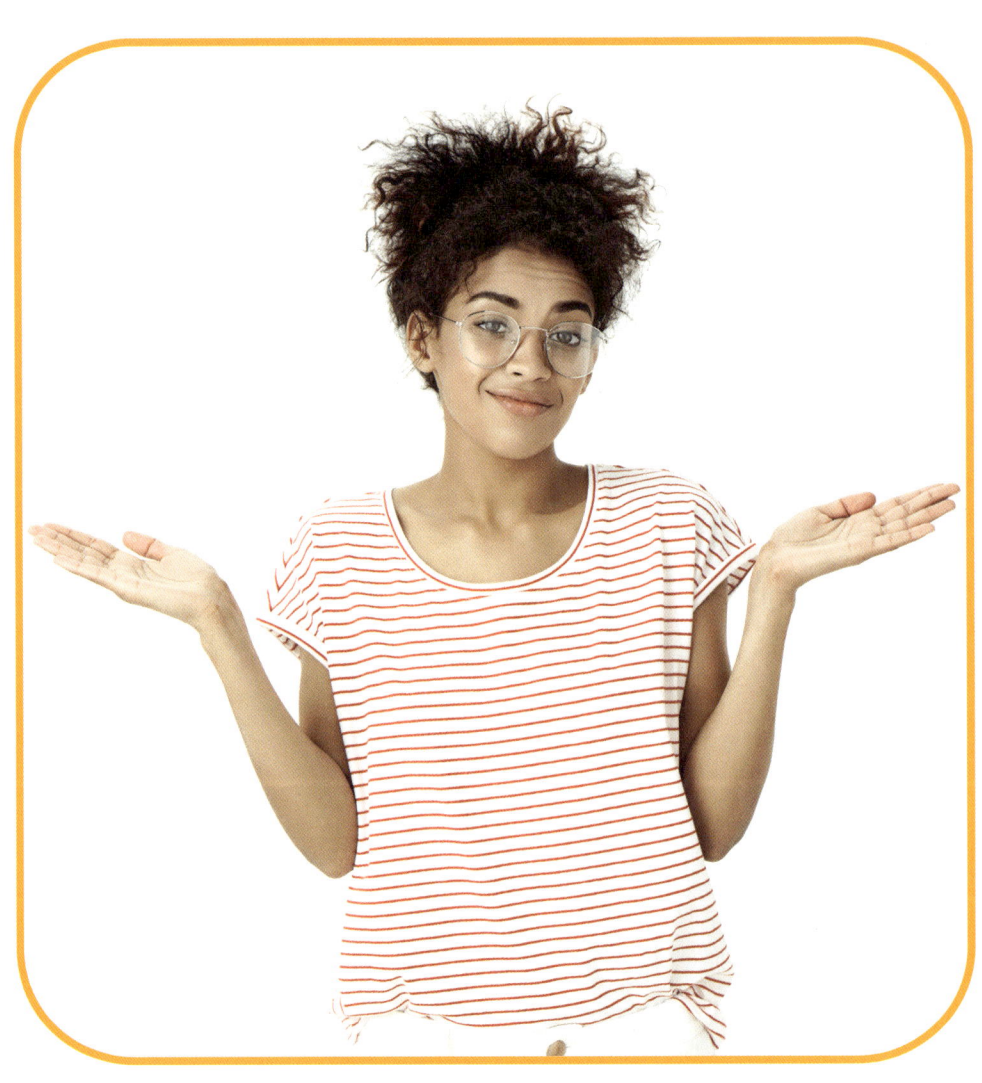

how

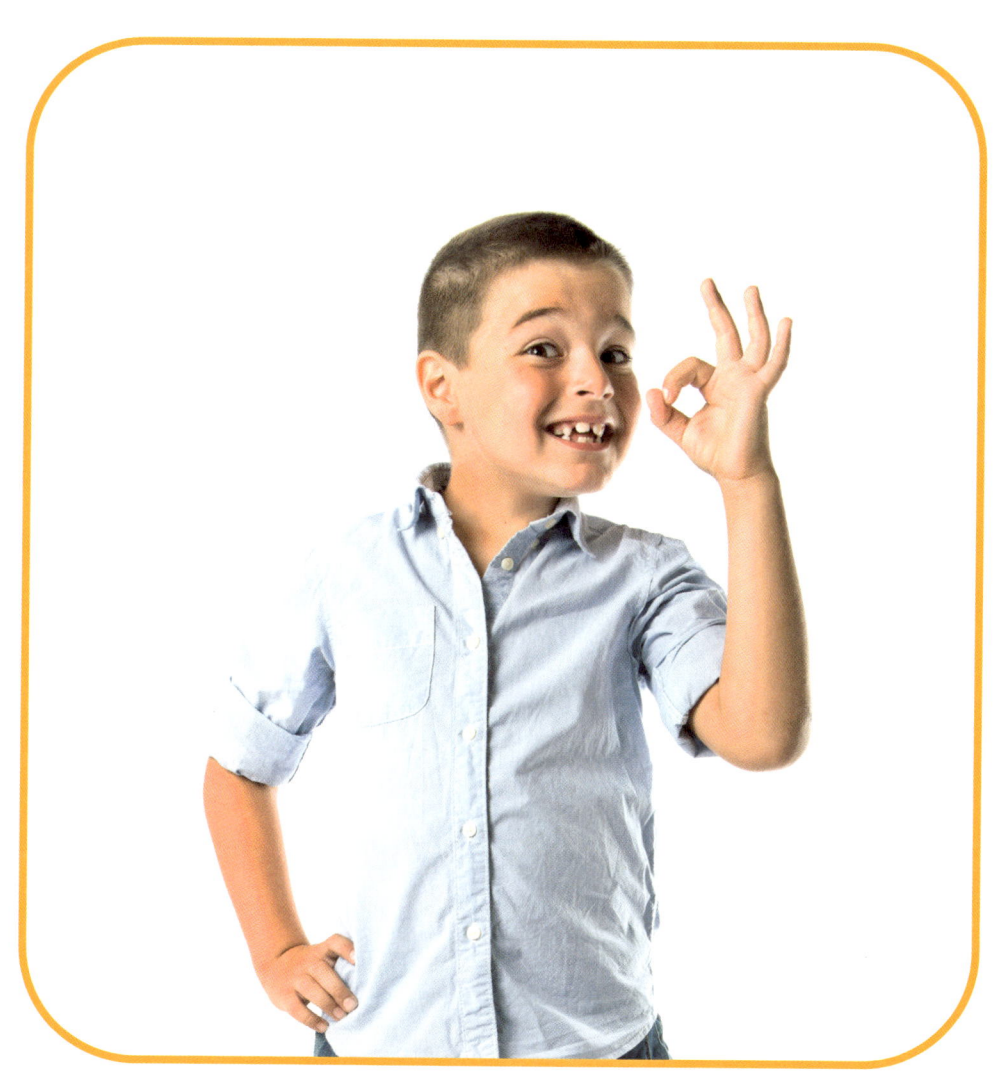

fine

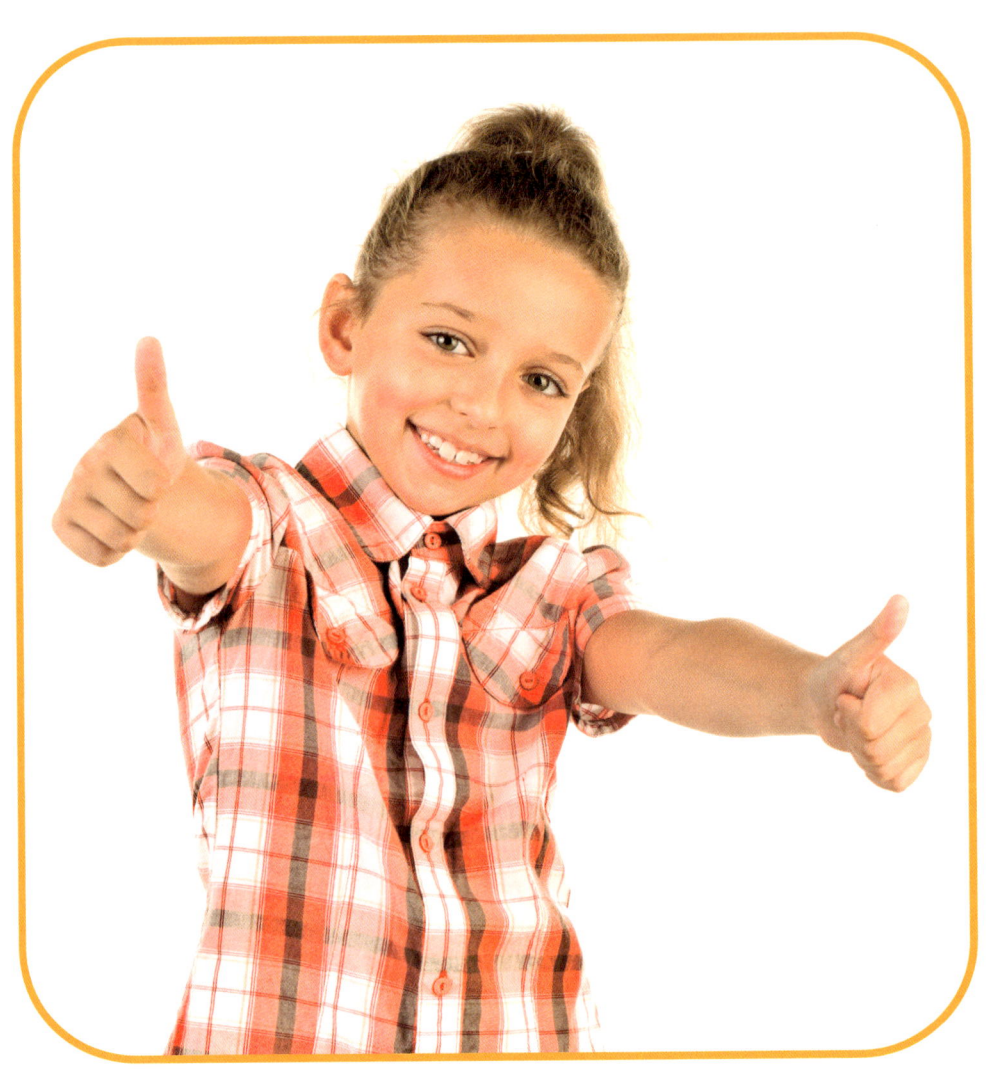

great

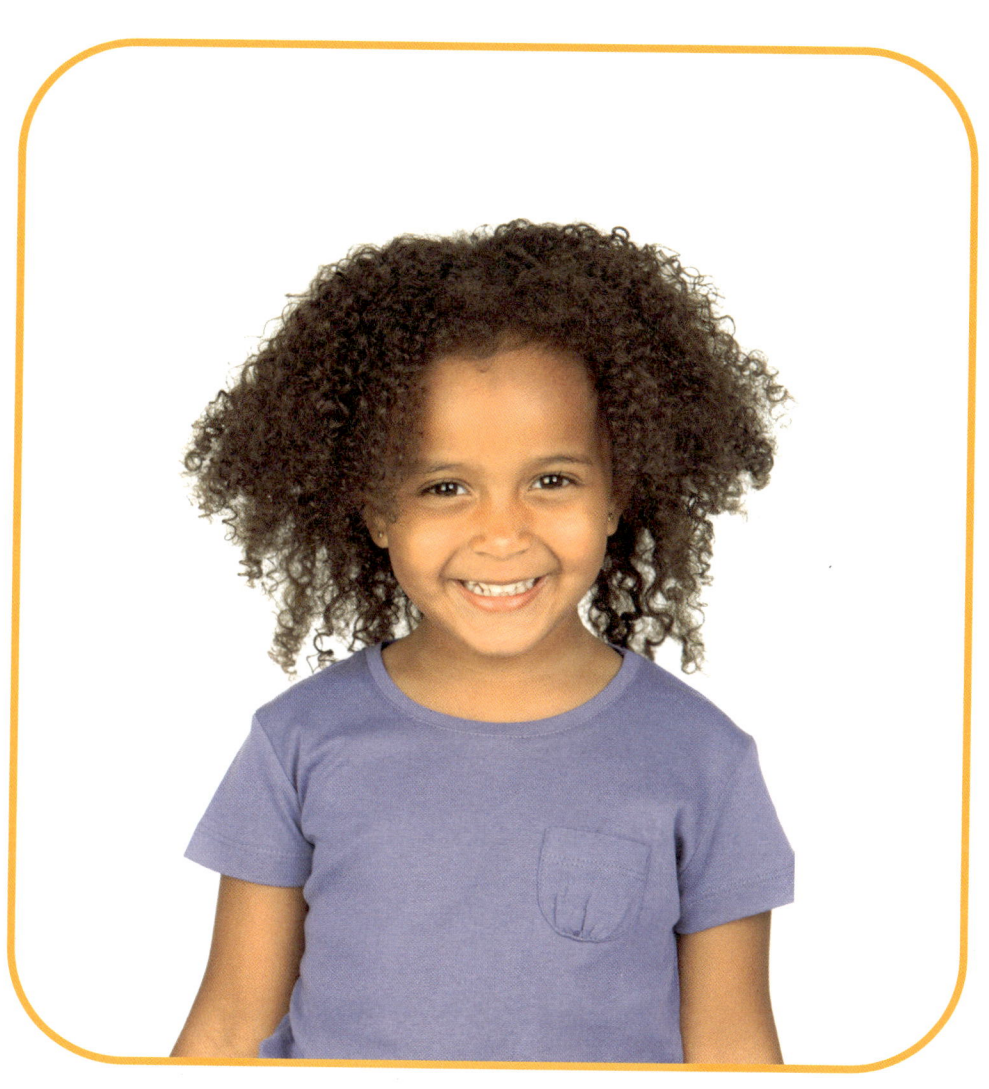

happy

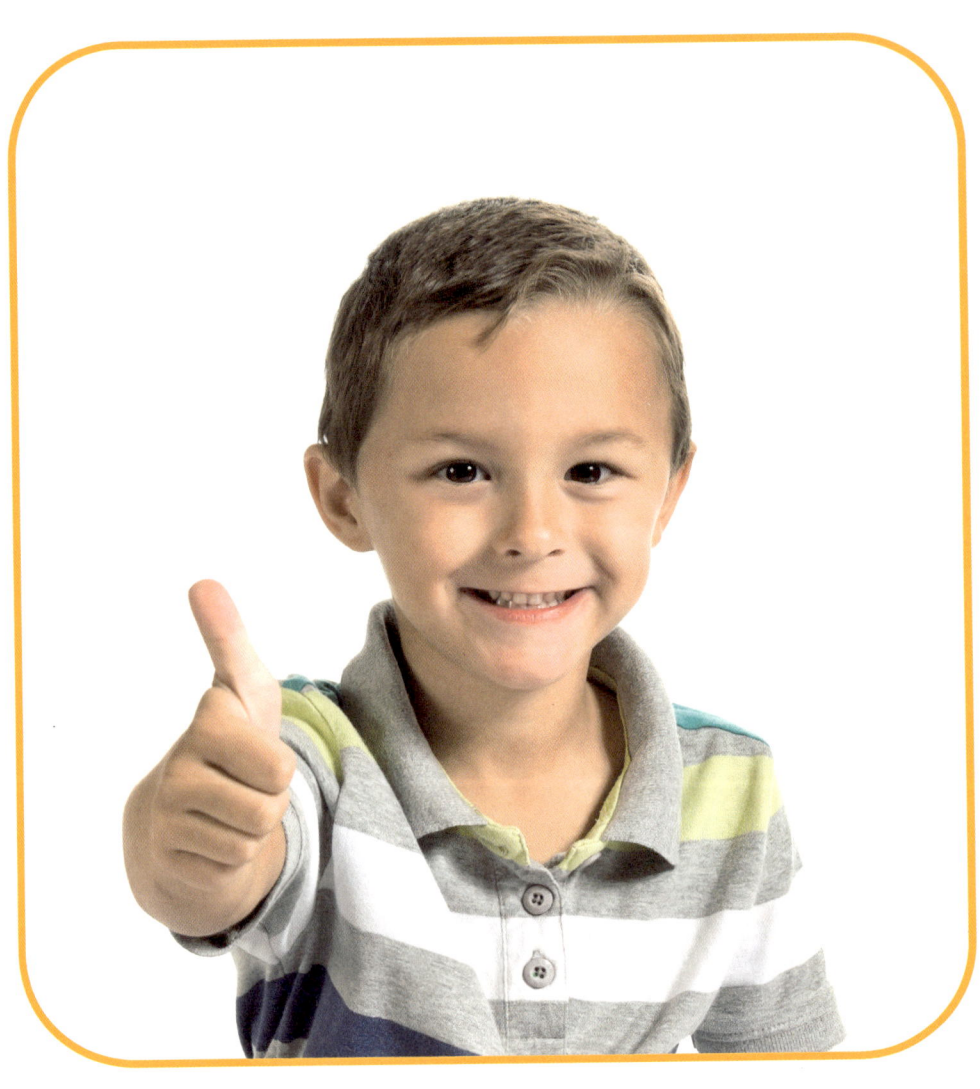

good

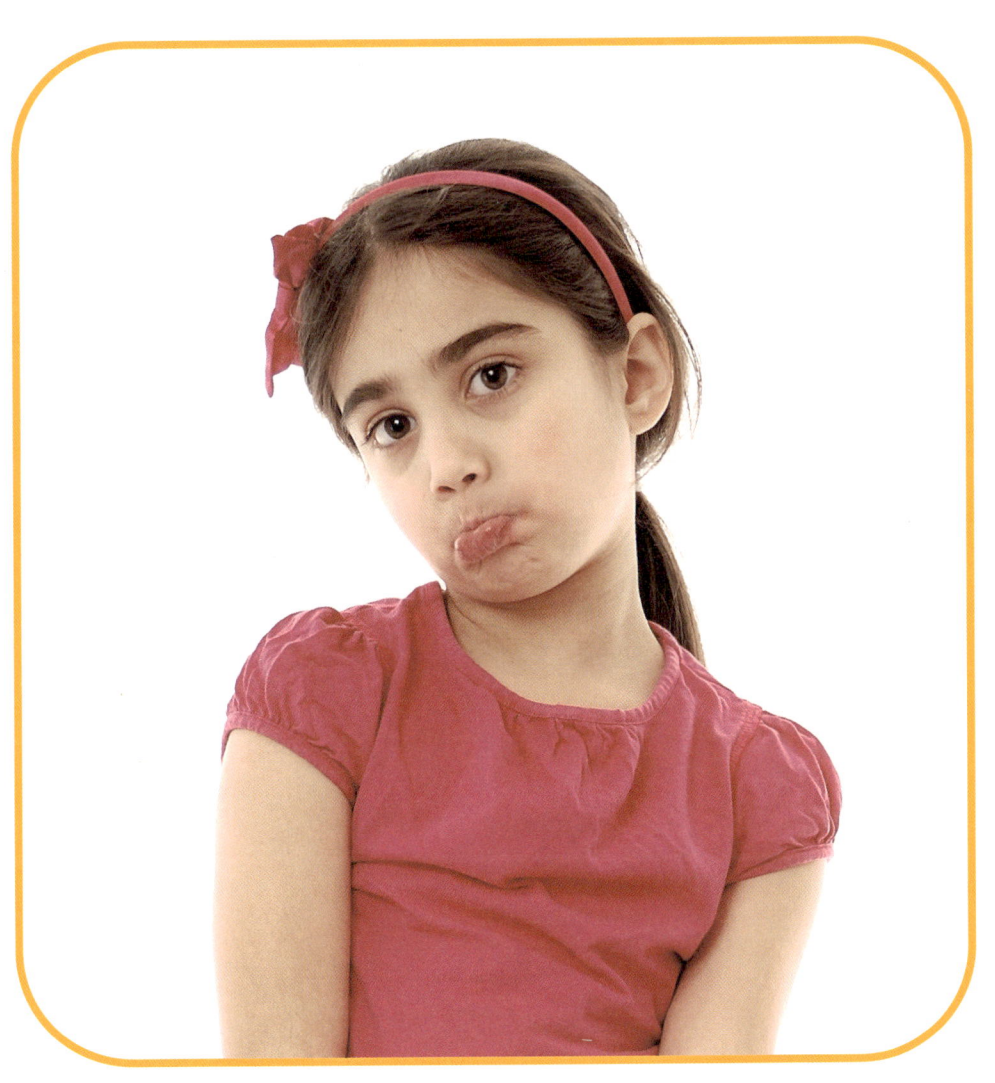

sad

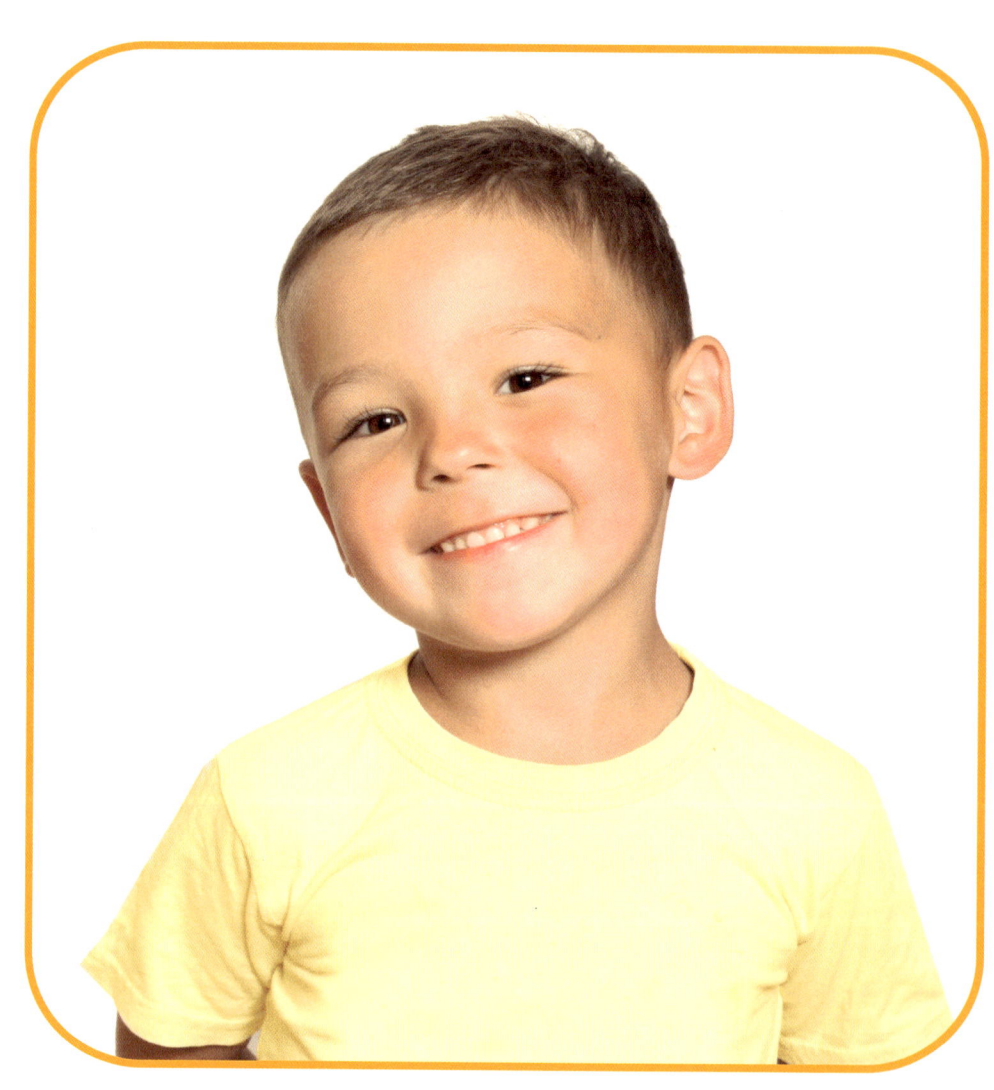

How are you,
Mom?

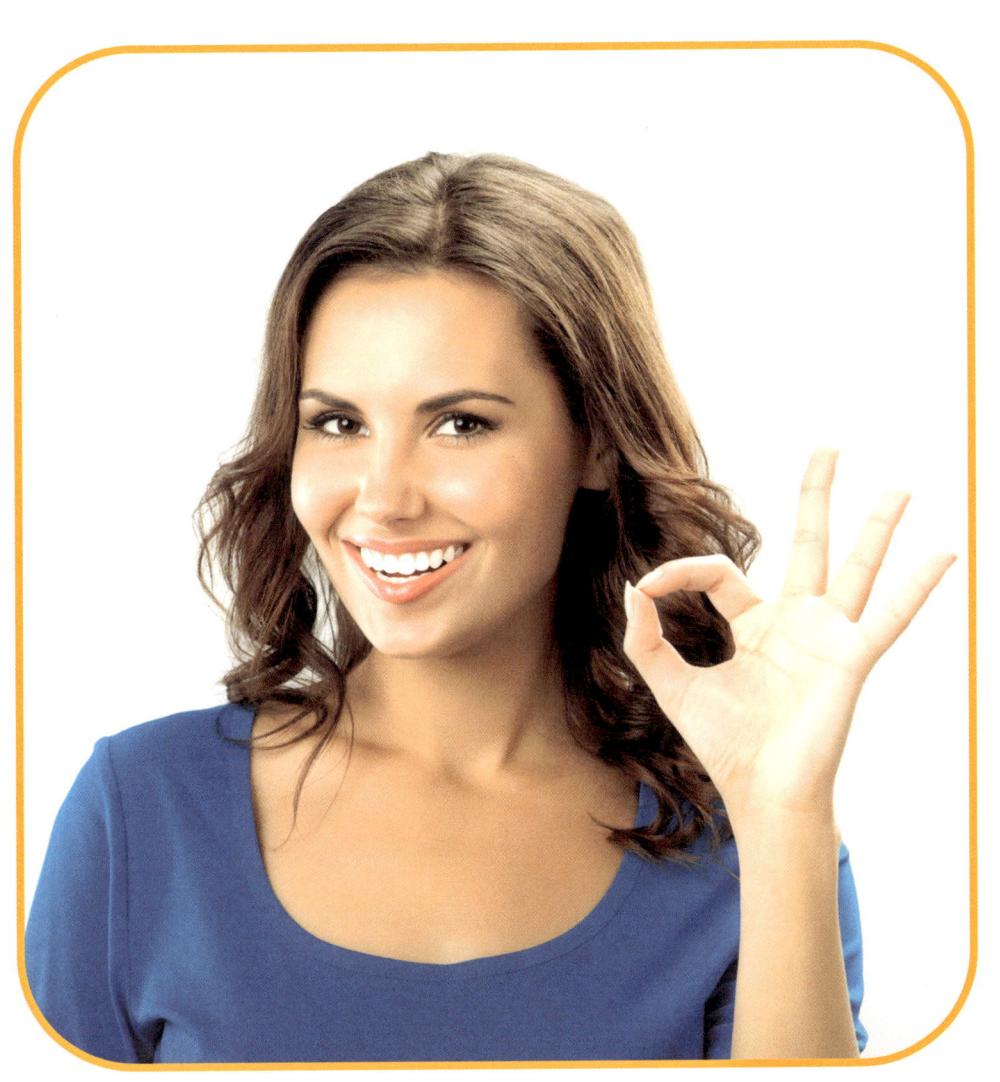

I am fine.

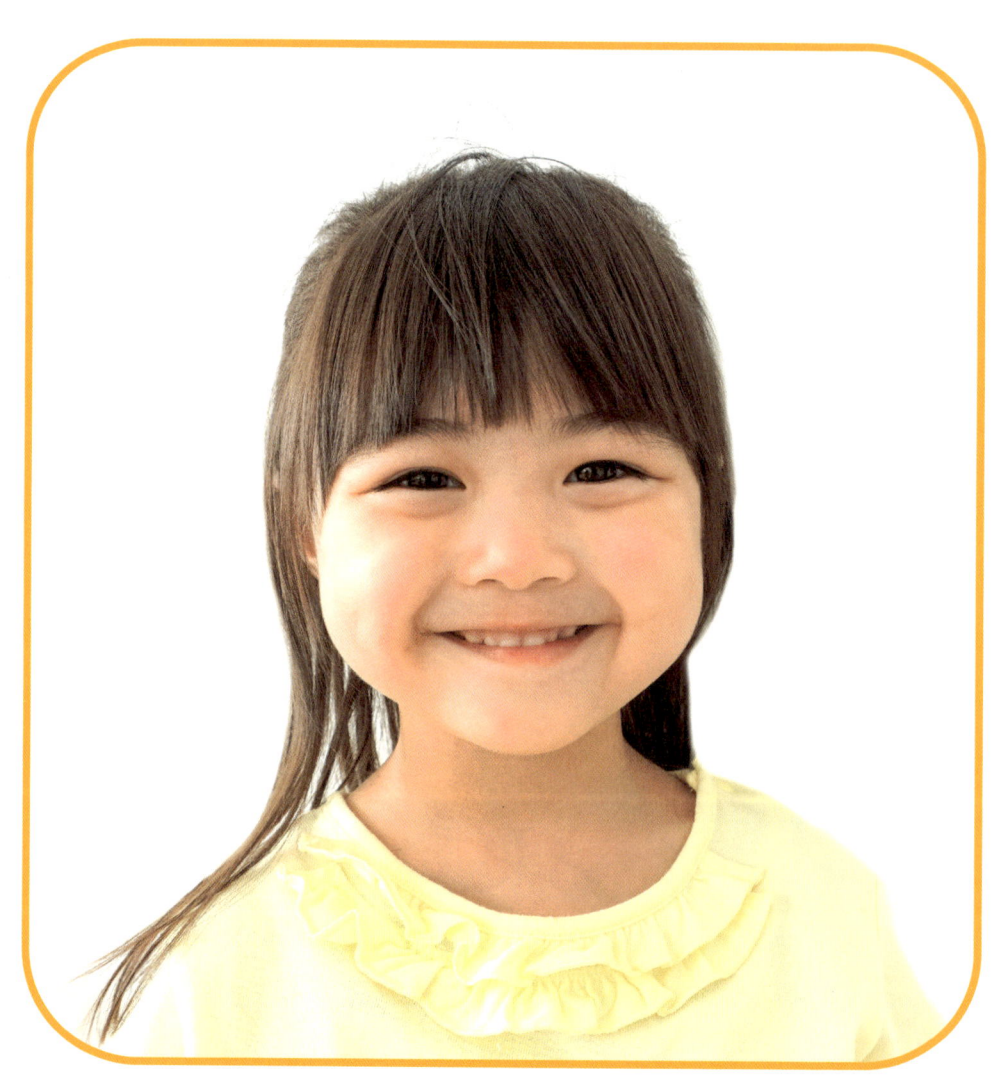

How are you, Dad?

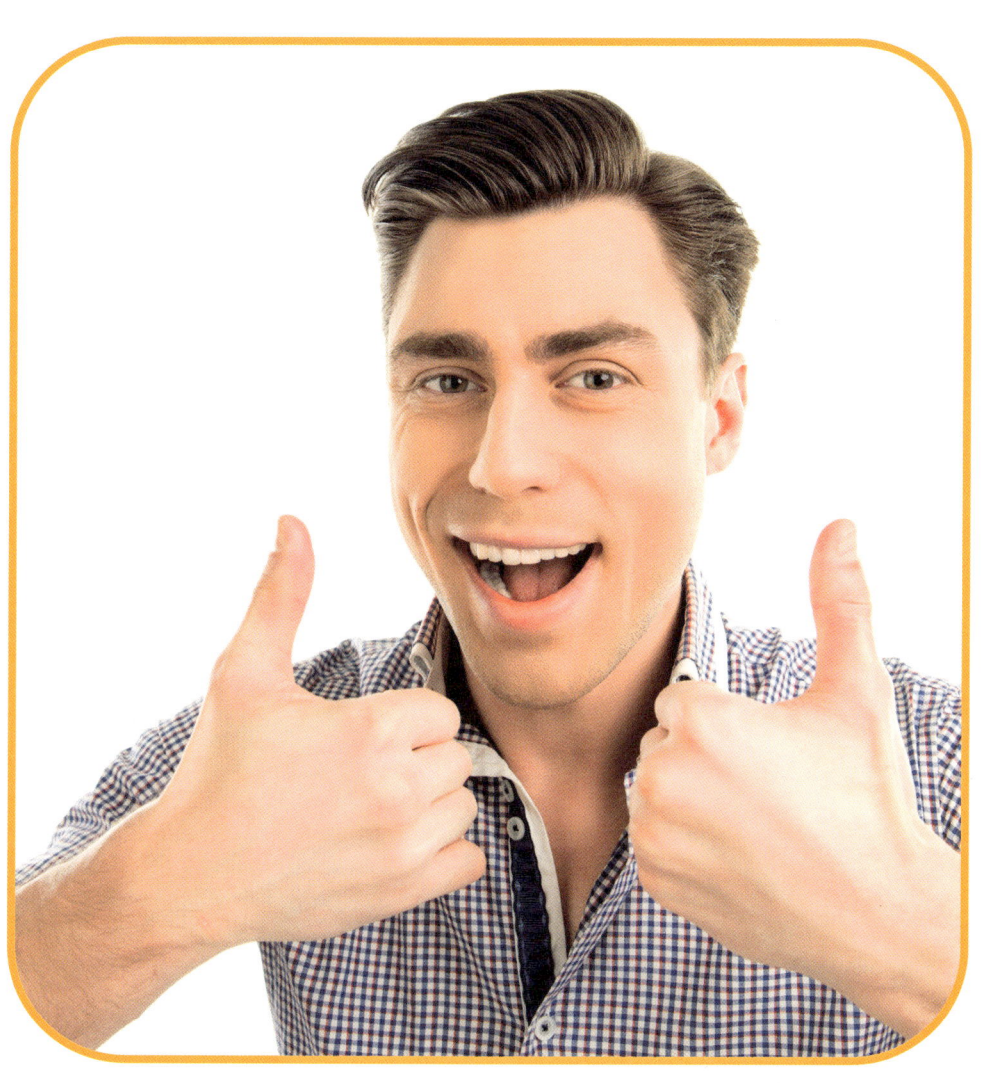

I am great.

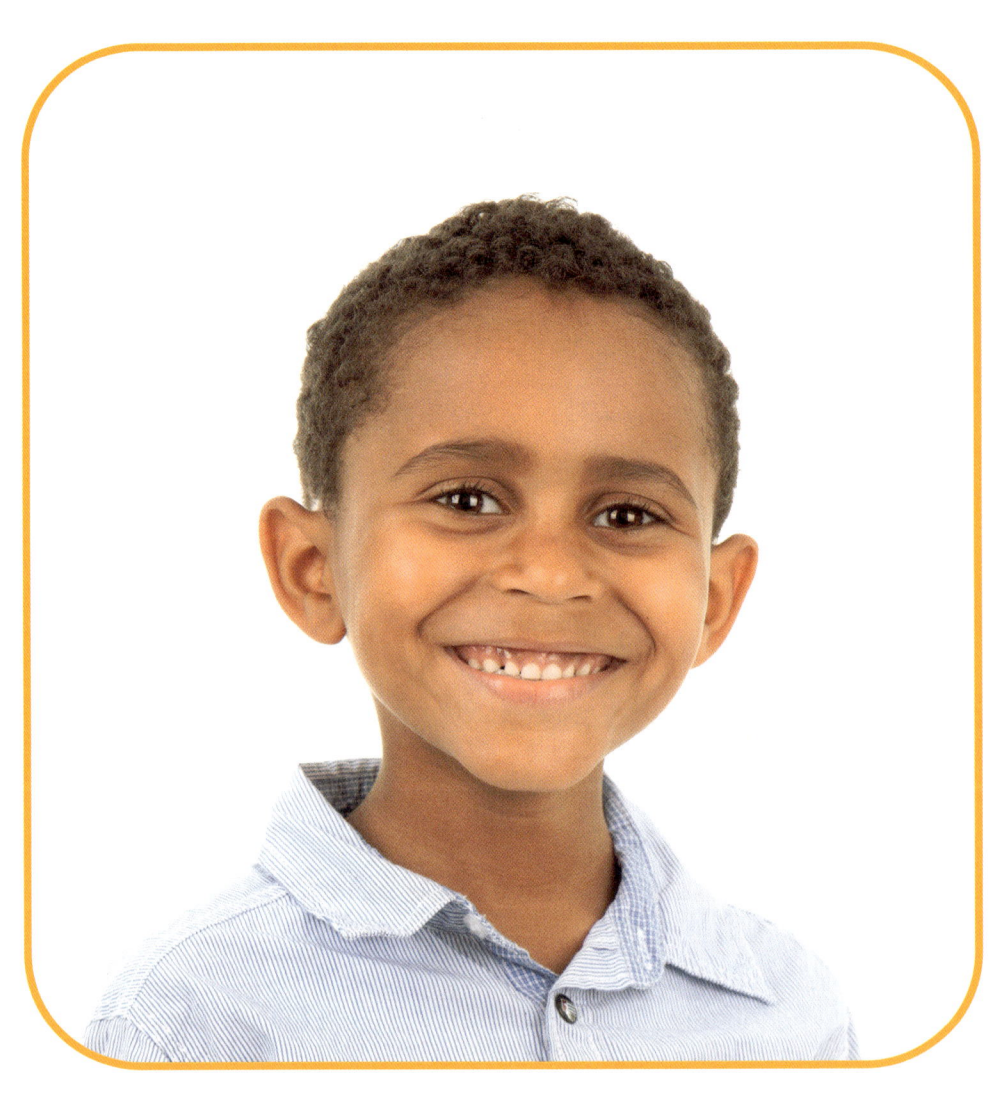

How are you,
Teacher?

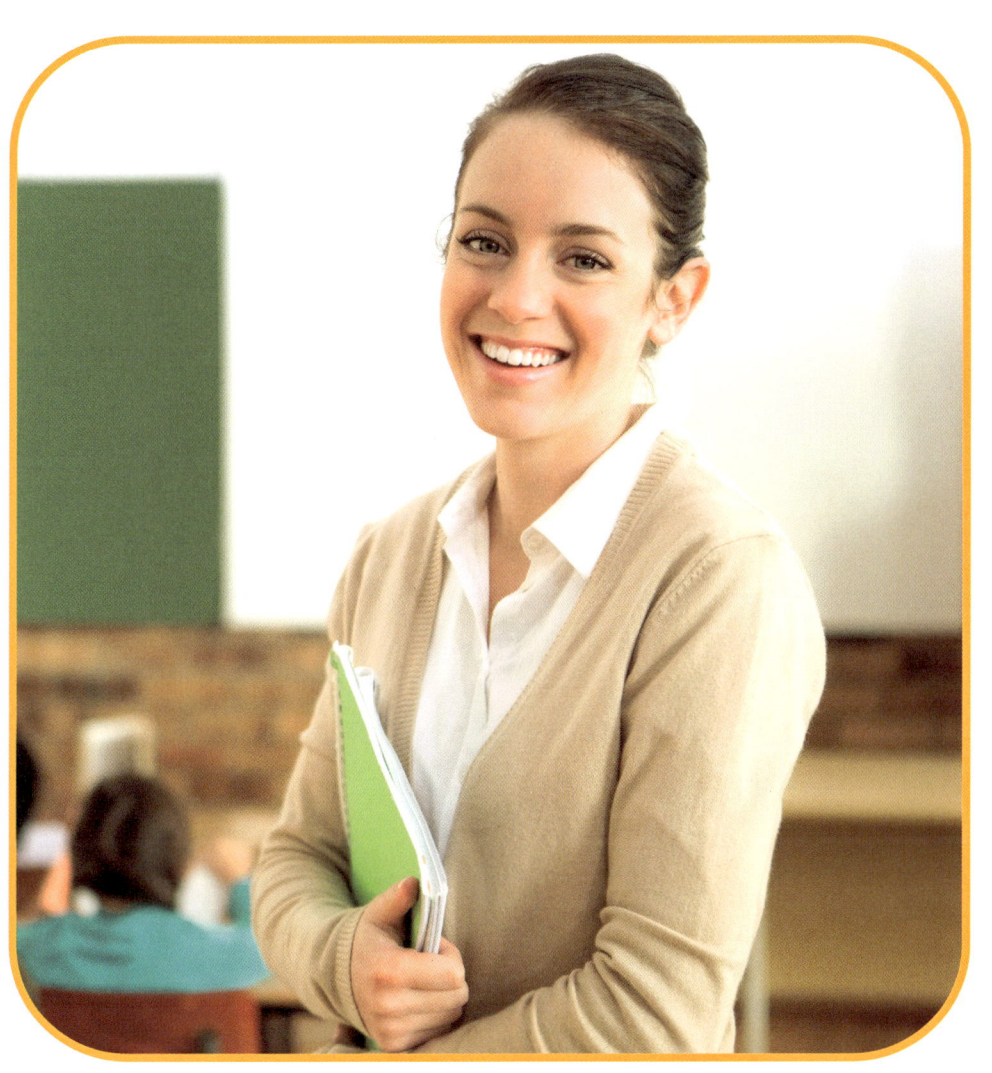

I am happy.

Word List

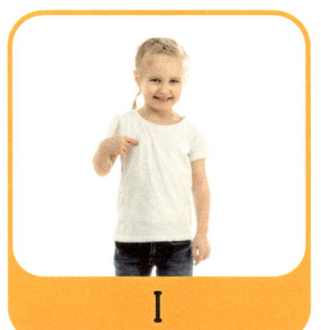

I

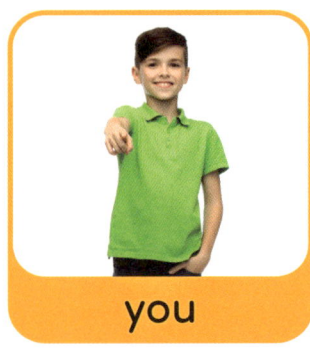

you

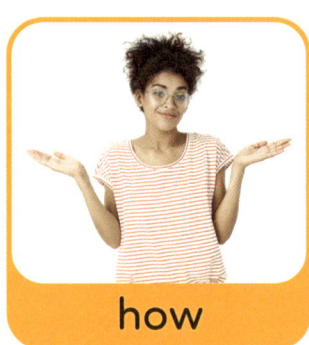

how

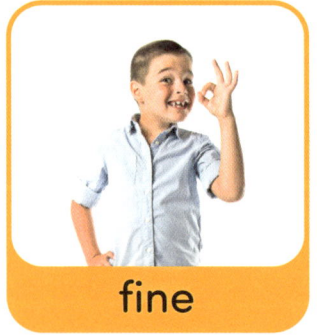

fine

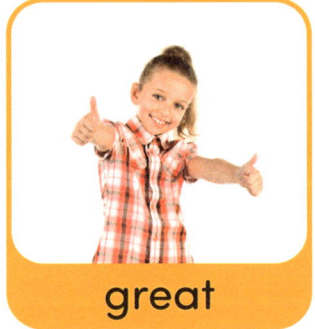

great

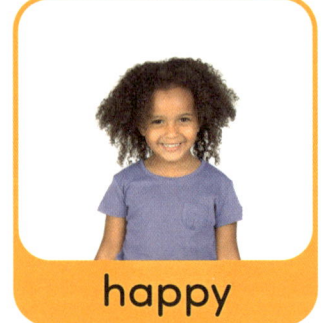

happy

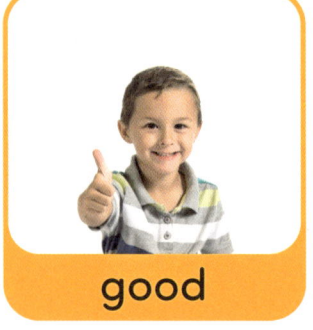

good

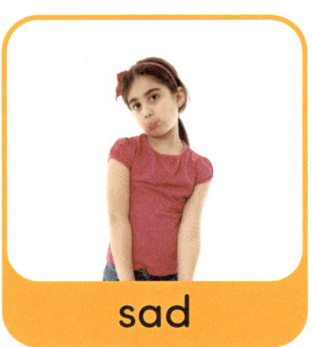

sad